ECHOES OF EMOTIONS

A Journey of Healing & Hope

VIVEK H SUTAR

ISBN 979-8-89026-685-9

Dedication

To ViRaj, whose poetry spoke the words I could not find, and whose spirit gave me the strength to heal. This book, 'Echoes of Emotions,' is a tribute to your inspiring journey and an ode to the power of words.

– Vivek H Sutar

Acknowledgement

Dear Reader,

Before you dive into the pages of this book, I wanted to take a moment to express my deepest gratitude to those who helped make it possible.

First and foremost, I want to thank my dear friend and designer extraordinaire- Prathamesh Kiran Patil. Your creativity and expertise brought my vision to life in ways I never thought possible. Your eye for design and attention to detail has taken this book to new heights; and for that, I am truly grateful.

I would also like to extend my gratitude to the publishers who believed in this book from the very beginning. Your unwavering support and guidance throughout the publishing process have been invaluable, and probably I couldn't have done this without you.

Finally, to you, dear reader, I am truly humbled that you have chosen to pick up this book and are embarking on this journey with me. I hope that the words and stories within these pages move you, inspire you, and challenge you in new and in unexpected ways.

Thank you for joining me on this journey of healing, hope, and transformation.

Sincerely,

ViRaj

Contents

01

The Power of Resilience: Overcoming Trauma and Pain

I met a boy who taught me well,
Of strength and courage in his tale to tell,
he'd been through trauma, pain and strife,
And yet he stood, still full of life.

But little did I know back then,
That this boy was actually me, my friend,
I'd been through struggles just the same,
And yet I'd found a way to rise again.

Through tears I shared my darkest days,
And how I'd found a different way,
To see the world with open eyes,
And find the light amidst the lies.

My words they touched my heart so deep,
And opened up my eyes to see,
That gratitude towards humanity,
Is where we find our destiny.

For in this world of endless pain,
We need the strength to love again,
To see the beauty that's within,
And find the light that shines within.

let us walk this path with grace,
And spread warmness and love in every place,
For gratitude towards humanity,
Is where we find our destiny

02

The Transformative Power of Love

Love, a force so pure,
Its power we can't ignore.
It heals, it inspires,
And fills our hearts with desires.

But love can also hurt,
Leaving scars that won't revert.
We must tread with care,
And be true, loving and fair.

For love is not just a feeling,
But a choice, a conscious dealing.
It requires patience, sacrifice,
And the courage to pay the price.

So, let us love with all our might,
And make our world a little bright.
For love, in its truest form,
Has the power to transform.

03

The Healing Power of Words: ViRaj's Story

A broken heart, a shattered soul,
ViRaj once had a life so whole.
But then she came, and everything changed,
His world turned upside down, rearranged.

The trauma hit him hard, it's true,
And nothing he could do, or pursue.
His academics, his projects, his dreams,
All seemed to slip away, it seems.

The sweet chats and quarrels they had,
Were the only things that made him glad.
Her presence in his life, a newfound meaning,
But now she's gone, leaving him grieving.

In classrooms, he would cry,
And his pain he'd try to pacify,
With pen and paper, he would compose,
Poems that expressed his woes.

The world didn't understand, nor care,
Why he was lost in his despair.
They judged and accused him, without a thought,
And forced him to a mental hospital, distraught.

Even his family, once so proud,
Left him alone, in his pain, to drown.
But through it all, ViRaj kept on writing,
His words, his solace, his only guiding.

For in his words, he found his peace,
His broken heart, he could release.
He taught us all, that in life's darkest hour,
Writing can be our saving power.

So, let us not judge, nor condemn,
Those who suffer, beyond our ken.
Instead, let us lend a listening ear,
And help them heal, and conquer their fear.

For ViRaj's story, though tragic and sad,
Teaches us to be kind, and never bad.
And in the end, he left us a gift,
A lesson in love, and how to uplift.

04

Shadows Within: A Journey of Healing and Hope

The shadows within, they cloud my mind
A weight that's heavy, almost unkind
They whisper secrets, dark and deep
And rob me of my peaceful sleep

I try to shake them, with all my might
But they cling to me, both day and night
The stigma's heavy, hard to bear
A burden that's not mine to share

I wish for light, to break the dark
To heal the wounds, leave just a mark
But the journey's long, the path unclear
A road I walk, filled with fear

The shadows within, they won't let go
But still, I fight, and take it slow
With each small step, I find some peace
And with each breath, the pain does ease

So if you too, know this plight
Please know, it's okay to fight
The shadows may be here to stay
But in the light, we'll find our way

05

Aura Through Darkness

In darkness I sit, consumed by sorrow's flame,
A sadness that lingers, like a shadow with no name.
Silent hours pass, with no solace to be found,
As I endure this pain, that wears my soul down.

The light of day is gone; replaced by endless night,
And I am left alone, with nothing but my fright.
No phone, no TV, nothing to break the still,
Just my thoughts and tears, in this room, so chill.

My heart is heavy, with a weight I can't explain,
And I am left to wonder, WHAT has caused this pain.
Is it the passing of time, or the choices I've made?
Or is it simply fate, that I can never evade?

I know I must move on, but the road ahead is steep,
And I am lost in thought, as I try to catch some sleep.
But in this dark abode, where my soul feels so light,
I find a glimmer of hope, in this endless night.

So I will hold on tight, to this small ray of light,
And I will face the day, with all my might.
For though I am not well; & my heart aches with pain,
I know I will find my way, and rise from this insane.

06

Lessons in Personal Growth

In my dreams, I see myself as great
An achiever, a success, a master of fate
But in reality, the journey is long and slow
With many hurdles, lessons, and unknowns

Personal growth is no easy task
It requires courage, strength, and a will to last
To face our fears and embrace the unknown
And to learn from mistakes, no matter how prone

It's not just about achieving success or fame
But about becoming the best version of our name
To grow and evolve, with every step we take
And to never let setbacks, our spirit break

To grow, we must let go of old ways
And open our hearts to new rays
To trust the journey, and the process too
And to have faith that we'll make it through

So let's embrace the complexity of growth
And all the beauty that it does behold
For with each step, we become more whole
And with each lesson, we reach a new goal

07

The Weight We Bear : A Lesson in Understanding and Empathy

ViRaj, a soul so deep and true,
Misunderstood by all, but who knew?
The potential they saw, but not the pain,
Of a shattered heart, a soul in vain.

They pushed and prodded, demanded and begged,
For him to perform, to excel, to be ahead.
But little did they know, the weight he bore,
The burden of trauma, a life so sore.

In classrooms, he would sit and write,
Words that flowed, with all his might.
His only escape, from a world so cruel,
Where judgment and misunderstanding, were the rule.

They saw his talent, his gift of words,
But failed to see the pain, that soared like birds.
They urged him on, to achieve and succeed,
But left his heart, in a state of need.

ViRaj, a lesson to be learned,
That understanding and empathy, cannot be earned.
For every person, has a story to tell,
A life of pain, that they bear so well.

So, let us listen, with open ears,
And wipe away, each other's tears.
For in understanding, we find our peace,
A world of love, where judgment, can cease.

Let us not push, or demand and beg,
For we know not, the weight they bear, that they drag.
Instead, let us lift, with a gentle hand,
And show them, a world so grand.

ViRaj, a soul, we will not forget,
For in his words, we found our safety net.
A lesson, we will hold dear,
To love and understand, and never fear.

08

Beyond Reality

Imagination, oh what a gift,
A power that can give us a lift,
A tool that helps us see beyond,
And find solutions we thought were gone.

With just a thought, we can create,
A world so vivid and innate,
A place where dreams can come alive,
And anything is possible to strive.

Imagination is a key,
To unlock the doors we cannot see,
A way to break free from the mold,
And let our minds and spirits unfold.

It takes us to places far and wide,
Beyond what reality can provide,
To galaxies, kingdoms, and magical lands,
Where we can be anything, with no demands.

So let your imagination soar,
And let it open every door,
For in its depths, you'll find a treasure,
That will bring you joy, beyond all measure.

09

Belonging Together:
A Proposal of Love

In every breath that I take,
And every move that I make,
I feel your presence, everywhere,
In the light, in the dark, in the air.

Your smile, your touch, your voice,
They make my heart skip, they give me poise.
I cannot imagine a life without you,
For you make me whole, you make me new.

So, my love, I have a question to ask,
One that's been burning in me, an urgent task.
Will you be my partner, my soulmate, my all?
Will you walk with me, in life's rise and fall?

I promise to cherish you, to love you true,
To stand by your side, no matter what we go through.
Together, we'll write our own beautiful story,
Filled with love, passion, and glory.

So, my dearest one, please say you'll be mine,
And we'll embark on this journey, divine.
For my heart, my soul, my life,
Belong to you, my beloved wife.

10

Echoes of Emotion

In the silence of my heart,
Echoes of emotion start,
A symphony of joy-pains,
That flows through my veins.

Memories of love and loss,
Moments of triumph and toss,
All intertwined in a dance,
That leaves me in a trance.

The depth of feeling is so strong,
It's hard to tell right from wrong,
But in the chaos, I can see,
The beauty of my humanity.

For every tear that I shed,
Every word left unsaid,
Is a testament to my soul,
A story waiting to unfold.

So let the echoes fill up the air,
Let the pain and joy be there,
For it's in these emotions deep,
That I find the strength to keep.

11

The Profound Journey: Embracing Life's Twists & Turn

I've walked a path both light and dark
Through valleys low and mountains stark
And in the end, what I have found
Is that the journey is profound

I've learned that life is not a race
But rather, it's a sacred space
To love and learn, to laugh and cry
And to embrace each moment before it passes by

I've learned that joy is not in things
But in the happiness that living brings
And that the greatest gift of all
Is the love we give, both big and small

I've learned that challenges can be tough
But they help us grow, they make us tough
And that with each step we take in life
We're one step closer to ending strife

So when I look back on my journey
I'm grateful for every twist and turn-y
For in each moment, I found a gift
And in each step, my spirit did lift.

12

Radiate : The Power of Self-Care

In the rush of life, it's easy to forget
The importance of self-care, and what it begets
We put others first, and neglect our own needs
And wonder why we're depleted, with hearts that bleed

But self-care is not a luxury, it's a necessity
A way to nourish ourselves, with love and intensity
It's not selfish, it's self-love, and it's what we all deserve
To tend to our own garden, and let our inner beauty
preserve

Self-care is not just bubble baths and spa days
It's also setting boundaries, and saying no in many
ways
It's taking time to rest, and to recharge our soul
To connect with our inner wisdom, and to make
ourselves whole

Self-care is not always easy, it's a journey of growth
To face our fears and insecurities, and to learn to cope
It's a process of learning to love ourselves, flaws and all
To accept ourselves unconditionally, and to stand tall

So let's make self-care a priority, each and every day
To nurture our mind, body, and spirit in every way
For when we care for ourselves,
we shine our brightest light
And radiate love and joy, with all our might.

13

Midnight Dreams of Love & Dance

In the midnight hours, my mind takes flight
And in my dreams, I see my greatest height
My VGOC, the world's best
An empire of excellence, innovation and quest

And in that moment, as I stand on the stage at AGM
A love like ours, that nothing can ever stem
I see you in the crowd, smiling and bright
My heart swells with pleasure, with all its might

I remember the days, when we danced at college
And now in my dreams, with you as my solace
I can't help but imagine, how it would feel
To dance with you again, with nothing to conceal

My love, you are the one who makes me complete
And in my dreams, our dancing is such a sweet feat
I thank the stars above, for you in my life
For being my partner, my soulmate, my wife

So here's my proposal, my love, will you dance with me?
Through all of life's challenges, with you, I'm free
With you by my side, I know we'll achieve it all
Let's dance through life, until the final curtain call.

14

A Journey Through Time

The past is a tale, a story we share
Of who we were and how we did fare
It's a roadmap of where we've been
A teacher of lessons deep within

The present is a chance, a moment to seize
To love, to laugh, and to be at ease
It's an opportunity to be present and aware
To create a life beyond compare

The future is a puzzle, a path yet untold
A destination we hope to unfold
It's a canvas for us to paint our vision
A reality we can shape with precision

The past, present, and future all converge
A tapestry woven with love and courage
The past echoes through the present, the present
guides the future
Together, a divine melody to nurture

So cherish the past, embrace the present
And trust the future, for it's not yet spent
For in this interplay of time and space
Lies the beauty of life, its mystery and grace

15

Moments Carried By the River of Time

As the river of time flows on and on
It carries with it moments that are gone
Like a rushing current, it races by
With each passing second, a precious butterfly

So delicate and fleeting, it flits and flies
And though we grasp, it eludes our tries
For time takes flight, with every sunrise
Leaving us with memories that may suffice

A sculptor, time shapes us with each event
With every surprise, a new layer is spent
A chisel sharp, it cuts and chips away
And from our lives, it carves the price we pay

A mirror to our soul, time reflects our fate
A reminder that life is never too late
A journey that we all must undertake
A path that leads to the final wake

With each step we take, time tries to outrun
Like a marathon that's just begun
But we must remember, with each passing day
That our time is precious, and not to throw away

So let us live each moment to the fullest
And embrace each experience, as we must
For time may be a mystery untold
But its value, worth more than gold.

Let this wisdom be our guide
To cherish each moment, side by side
For in the end, it's not the length of time
But the depth of life, that makes it sublime.

16

Love in the Midst of Healing

In the midst of healing, ViRaj met a girl named Alisha,
A neighbor's daughter, immature and sweet, like a fever.
As she visited her hometown, she began
following him online,
Alisha's messaging was constant,
which ViRaj took as a sign.

Despite ViRaj's warning that she would
fall in love with him,
Alisha refused to take it seriously,
thinking it was just a whim.
Until one day, she was so unhappy that she
poured out her heart,
And ViRaj, the wise poet, gave her guidance to
make a new start.

Alisha shared everything with ViRaj,
even her most private concerns,
And over time, she became so close to him,
it was a concern.
She would talk to him all day long, about
anything and everything,
And though she loved him, she never mentioned a thing.

Alisha treated ViRaj like a husband,
sending him pictures and jokes,

Her messages were constant, like a boat that never
stops, never chokes.

During the Ganesha festival, she acted as his
partner with devotion,

Messaging him 20 hours a day, as if it were a
marital notion.

Despite her feelings, ViRaj was still hurting,
and she didn't seem to know,

And though Alisha was a bright light,
she didn't understand his woe.

For ViRaj was still struggling, and
Alisha was just a distraction,

He was still healing from his trauma,
trying to find satisfaction.

So even though Alisha was his light,
ViRaj had to let her go,

For he needed to heal on his own, and
Alisha couldn't know.

She had brought him joy and laughter,
but ViRaj was still in pain,

And in the end, Alisha's love could not
make him whole again.

17

Festivals: A Flicker of Hope Amidst Life's Chaos

Amidst the chaos of life and the struggles,
A flicker of hope that never dwindles,
Comes in the form of festivals we celebrate,
A chance to rejoice and to alleviate.

In these moments of shared joy, happiness & laughter,
We find a respite from all that we're after,
A reminder of the good that still exists,
And the love that can still persist.

By the rhythms of music and dance,
And the tastes of food like kheer and
puran-poli that we enhance,
We find a sense of belonging and community,
A feeling of togetherness and unity.

These festivals carries the power,
To heal the soul in its darkest hour,
To light a path towards a brighter tomorrow,
And help us conquer all our sorrow.

For in these moments of collective mirth,
We find the strength to heal and unearth,
A spirit that refuses to be broken,
And a resolve that remains unshaken.

So let us celebrate these festivals with fervor,
And cherish the memories that they do uncover,
For in these moments of love and peace,
Lies the hope for a better world to release.

18

Biggest Fortune - The Blessing
of a Daughter

With joy beyond measure,
I welcome you, my daughter,
A precious gift of love that fills me with wonder,
In your eyes, I see the world anew,
A world of endless possibilities and dreams to pursue.

With every breath, I vow to cherish,
The bond we share, forever to nourish,
To protect and guide you,
through all life's highs and lows,
To be there for you, wherever life goes.

In your tiny fingers, I see a world of potential,
A future bright, shining and essential,
A world where your voice and your heart matter,
A world where you can chase your dreams and
never shatter.

As I hold you in my arms, my heart swells with pride,
And I am filled with gratitude for the love you provide,
For the blessings you bring, the joy you share,
For the light you bring, the hope you bear.

And as a token of my gratitude,
I distribute gold, a symbol of our fortitude,
For you embody strength and grace,
A hope for a future that's blessed with a better place.

So welcome, my dear daughter, to this world so bright,
May your days be filled with love,
laughter, and delight,
May you find the courage to chase your dreams,
And may you be blessed with happiness that
forever beams.

19

Threads of Fate

In a world of machines and wires,
I walked alone with my desires,
Lost in thought, lost in space,
In the midst of the AI race.

But then, from behind, came a blow,
And I was struck, my body aglow,
I lay there, broken, bruised and torn,
My mind awhirl, my spirit forlorn.

And as I lay in the hospital bed,
A stranger came to me and said,
"It was Pari who brought you here,
She saved your life, she was sincere."

But I was lost in my own despair,
My heart aching, beyond repair,
For I had no one, no kin, no friend,
No one to guide me, to help me mend.

But Pari stayed by my side,
Day and night, she did abide,
She took me home, she gave me care,
She healed my wounds, she was always there.
Yet still, I couldn't find the words,
To thank her for what she had incurred,
For the pain she caused, and the love she gave,
For the future lost, and the life she saved.

So I wrote, in the silence of the night,
Words that pierced the soul, and shone bright,
Echoes of emotion, echoes of pain,
Echoes of hope, that would never wane.

And as I wrote, my heart opened up,
And I saw Pari, not as my foe, but my prop,
She who had held me when I was weak,
She who had saved me when I couldn't speak.
And as I wrote, my words took flight,
Into the world, full of might,
They moved hearts, they touched souls,
They made the broken, once again whole.

And Pari read, with tears in her eyes,
The words that had once been my demise,
But now, they brought healing, they brought light,
And she saw in me, a different sight.

For I was not just a man, broken and lost,
But a poet, a prophet, who had paid the cost,
Of love and pain, of hope and despair,
Of life and death, and everything that's rare.
And Pari took over, with her heart full of love,
She completed my dreams, with the wings of a dove,
She built a company, that shook the world,
A company of love, of hope, of pearls.

And now, as I look back, from where I stand,
I see the beauty, of Pari's helping hand,
I see the love, that she always had,
I see the hope, that she never let go of.

And so, I write, with a heart full of grace,
With a pen that speaks, to every race,
With words that heal, and words that move,
With words that teach, and words that soothe.
For I am ViRaj, the poet, the seer,
The dreamer, who never let go of fear,
The lover, who found his way back,
The writer, who left his soul on the track.

Tears flow down my cheeks as I read this tale,
Of a broken man, and a love that did prevail,
Of a journey through pain, and a path to redemption,
Of a heart that was healed, and a soul that found exemption.

This story moves me, in ways I cannot express,
It touches my heart, it relieves my distress,
For it speaks of a love, that never lets go,
Of a hope that endures, through every high and low.

And so, I stand in awe, of ViRaj's bravery,
Of Pari's kindness, and her unwavering loyalty,
For they showed us, that even in the darkest of days,
Love and hope can find a way, to light

20

Healing the Earth, Healing Ourselves

The Earth we call our home, so vast and wide,
With mountains, oceans, and forests that provide,
A haven for creatures big and small,
A sanctuary for life, a gift for all.

Yet we have taken it for granted, our planet green,
Pristine nature now a distant dream,
Pollution, deforestation, and climate change,
The scars of our actions, a legacy strange.

The air we breathe, the water we drink,
Contaminated by our careless brink,
Species lost, habitats destroyed,
Nature's cry for help ignored.

But it's not too late to make a change,
To take responsibility and rearrange,
To plant a seed of hope, to nurture and grow,
To heal the Earth, to let it glow.

Let's reduce, reuse, and recycle,
To minimize waste and the impact we stifle,
Let's conserve, protect, and restore,
To keep the balance, to keep the Earth pure.

For in the end, it's not just the Earth we save,
But the future we build, the legacy we pave,
For the generations to come, to inherit,
A planet that's healthy, a world that's merit.

So let's unite in this journey of green,
To heal the Earth, to fulfill our dream,
Of a world where nature thrives and survives,
And the beauty of life forever revives.

21

The Price of Ignoring Self-Care

My mind and body, a temple so strong
Full of potential, limitless and long
I've climbed the highest peaks, swam the vastest seas
But health, I've come to learn, brings me to my knees

Though I'm talented and skilled, with so much to give
It's my self-care that lets my spirit thrive
No amount of success can replace
The importance of wellness, at a steady pace

I've learned this hard lesson through pain and trial
Pushing myself to the brink, I lost my smile
Now I know, my worth lies in my health
A treasure beyond measure, the key to true wealth

So I prioritize, my mind and physical well-being
Caring for my soul and all its feelings
By doing so, my potential is unleashed
A force of nature, unbreakable and fully reached

So listen to me, dear ones, take my advice
Prioritize your health, for the greatest prize
Nothing is more precious than your vitality
A life of wellness, true quality and totality.

22

The Sea Within

As the sea churns and crashes on the shore,
My emotions rise and fall forevermore.
For the sea, it holds a power so grand,
A connection to my soul, like a guiding hand.

With each ebb and flow, my heart takes flight,
And memories rush in with all their might.
Of loves lost, and longings unfulfilled,
The sea, it knows, the depths of the heart unsealed.

A tempest of emotions, it stirs within,
Like waves that crash, and then begin again.
And in the depths, a yearning to be free,
To find my place in the vast, endless sea.

The sea, a mirror to my soul it seems,
Reflecting back, the hopes and dreams,
Of a life filled with love, and endless possibility,
A world where pain and longing can find their serenity.

And as the sea recedes into the night,
Its whispers echo, a soothing light,
Reminding me of the beauty within,
And the power of love, to heal and begin.

For like the sea, my heart will ebb and flow,
And like the tides, my emotions will come and go.
But with each crashing wave, a new dawn will arise,
And with it, the chance to embrace life's surprise.

So let the sea be a symbol of hope,
Of a future filled with love, and endless scope,
And let it guide us through our darkest days,
To a life filled with joy, and endless ways.

As the waves collide against the shore,
My emotions stir like never before.
The sea holds power, mighty and grand,
Connecting with my soul, like a guiding hand.

With every ebb and flow, my heart takes flight,
As memories flood in with all their might.
Of love lost, and longings unfurled,
The sea knows, and unseals my heart, uncurled.

A tempest of emotions, it roils within,
Like waves that crash, then start again.

And in its depths, a yearning to break free,
To find my place in the endless sea.

The sea, a mirror to my soul, it seems,
Reflecting back the hopes and dreams,
Of a life filled with love and possibility,
A world where pain and longing find serenity.

As the sea recedes into the night,
Whispers echo, a soothing light,
Reminding me of the beauty within,
And love's power to heal and begin.

For like the sea, my heart will ebb and flow,
And like the tides, my emotions come and go.
But with each crashing wave, a new dawn does rise,
And with it, the chance to embrace life's surprise.

So let the sea be a symbol of hope,
A future filled with love and endless scope.
Let it guide us through our darkest days,
To a life of joy and endless ways.

23

Finding Strength in Storm

When life's tempests rage without an end,
And misery and pain around us bend,
And hope seems like a dream afar,
A glimmer of light can shine like a star.

For in the darkness deep and wide,
A hidden strength we can abide,
Though the suffering may weigh us down,
We must be resilient, strong, and profound.

Like a ship that sails through tumultuous waves,
We must be brave, to destiny's call we must pave,
Though the winds may knock us down,
We must rise again and stand our ground.

For through the trials and tests we face,
We discover new truths and find our place,
And though the journey may seem never-ending,
We must keep on, with love as our guiding.

Like a phoenix rising from the ashes,
We must shed our hurts, and let go of clashes,
And though the scars may still remain,
They'll remind us of the strength we've gained.

So let us embrace the storms we meet,
And our hearts with grace let us replete,
For every step we take, we grow and transform,
Our past a tale, our future a norm.

In the end, it's not about the pain,
But about the growth and strength we obtain,
And though the road may seem steep and long,
We'll emerge resilient, with a heart that's strong.

For within us lies a light that glows,
A beacon of hope that forever flows,
And with each step, we'll find our way,
To a brighter, happier, and peaceful day.

So let go of the past, let it be,
And embrace the future, with a heart that's free,
For in the end, we'll find our way,
And our pain will be a memory, fading away.

24

Dare to Be Different

In a world that seeks conformity
It's easy to lose our identity
To blend in and follow the crowd
Ignoring the voice that speaks loud

But the power lies in our uniqueness
The traits that make us different from the rest
The quirks and flaws we try to hide
Are what make us stand out with pride

Embrace your individualism
For it's what sets you free from the system
Don't fear the judgment or ridicule
For they're just tools to break the mold

Follow your heart and pursue your dreams
Even if they don't fit society's schemes
For in the end, it's your happiness that counts
And living on your own terms, paramount

So let go of the fear and doubts
And let your individualism speak out
For it's the key to true fulfillment
And living a life of contentment

Note: We intentionally left the last three pages of this book blank, inviting you to make this book your own. Whether it's a personal note, a poem, a drawing, or simply a list of your favorite quotes, we hope these blank pages offer you a space to reflect and create.